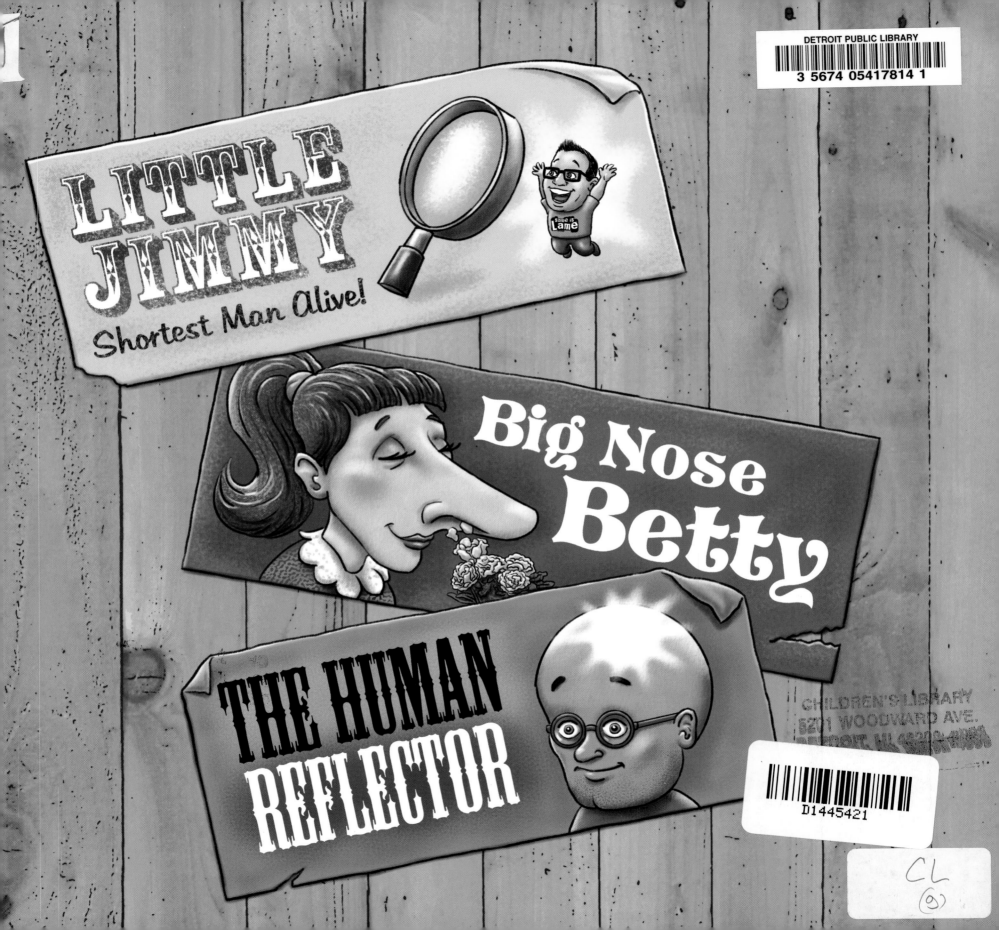

Autumn & Vin
Ella & Quinn
Allen & Aidan & Madelyn
Lucah & Rose & Mason (they're new)
William & Alex & Aiden (there's two)

Remember
this book,
I wrote it
for **you.**

Little Jimmy Says,

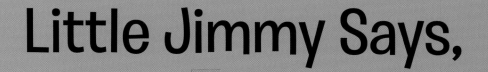

"Same Is Lame"

by Jimmy Vee

illustrations by Mike Motz

Edited by Allen J. Venezio

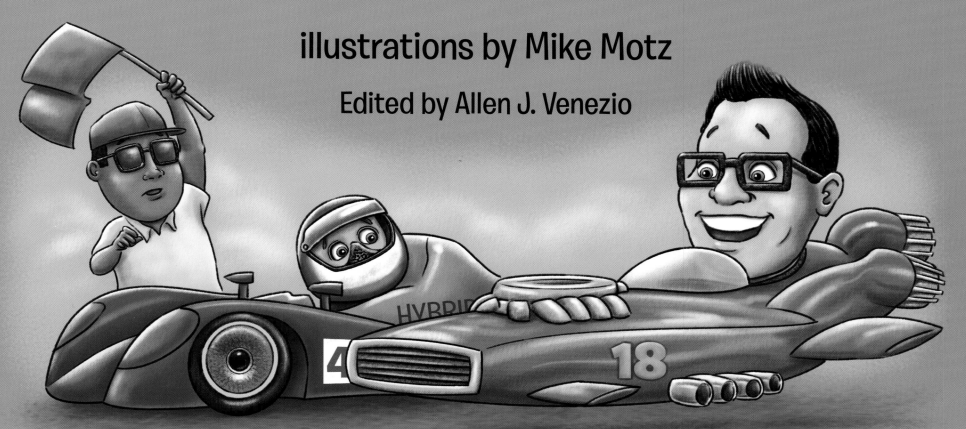

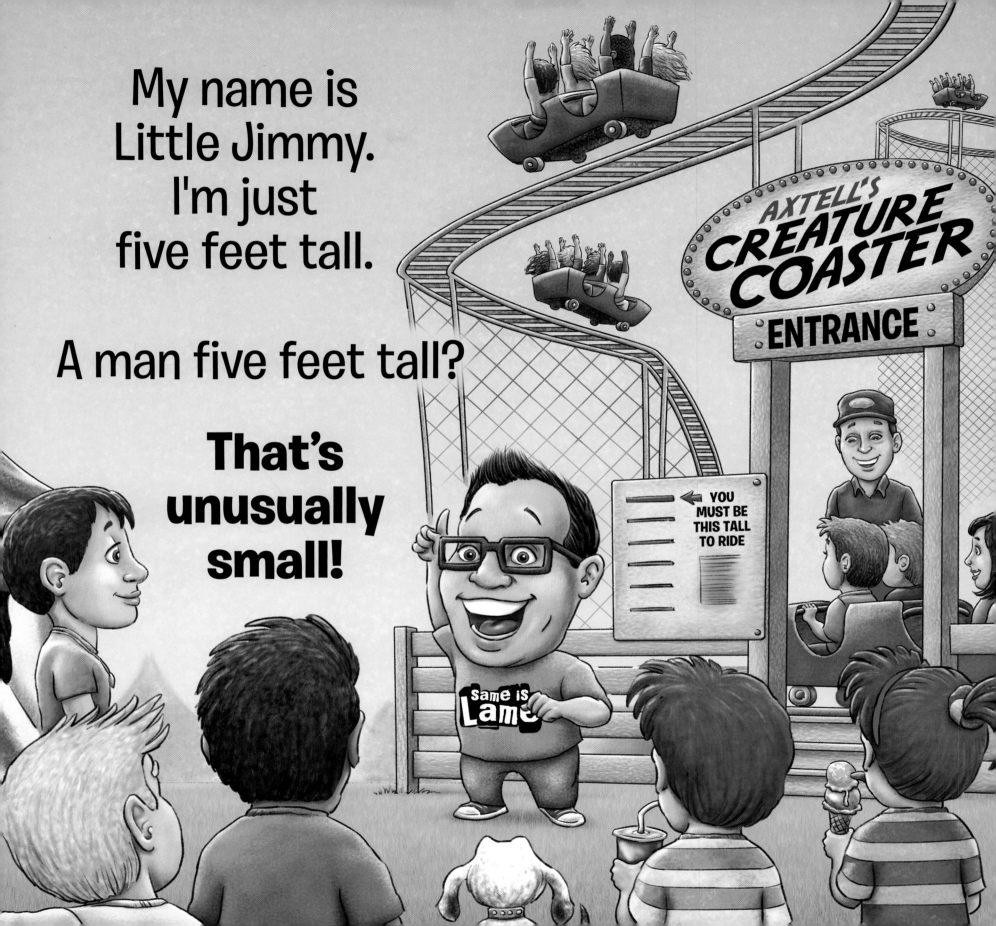

Let's play a game!
It will be lots of fun.

I think you will learn something when we are done.

Each person is different, as you will soon find.
Even you too. You are **one-of-a-kind!**

Tall people can hang pictures high up on the wall.

And some can **dunk** a basketball!

But being so **short** helps me do certain stuff that having long legs would make really tough.

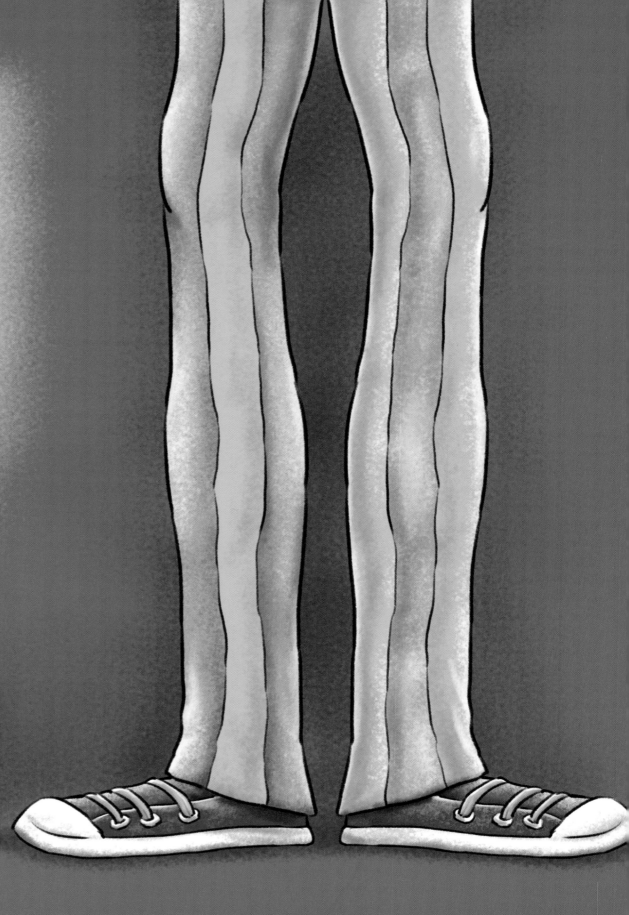

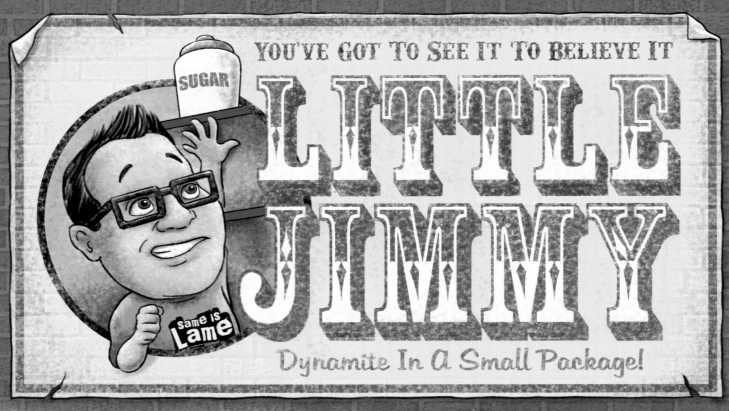

But, I can't reach the sugar, so am I a freak?

Of course not!

No Way!

It makes me **unique!**

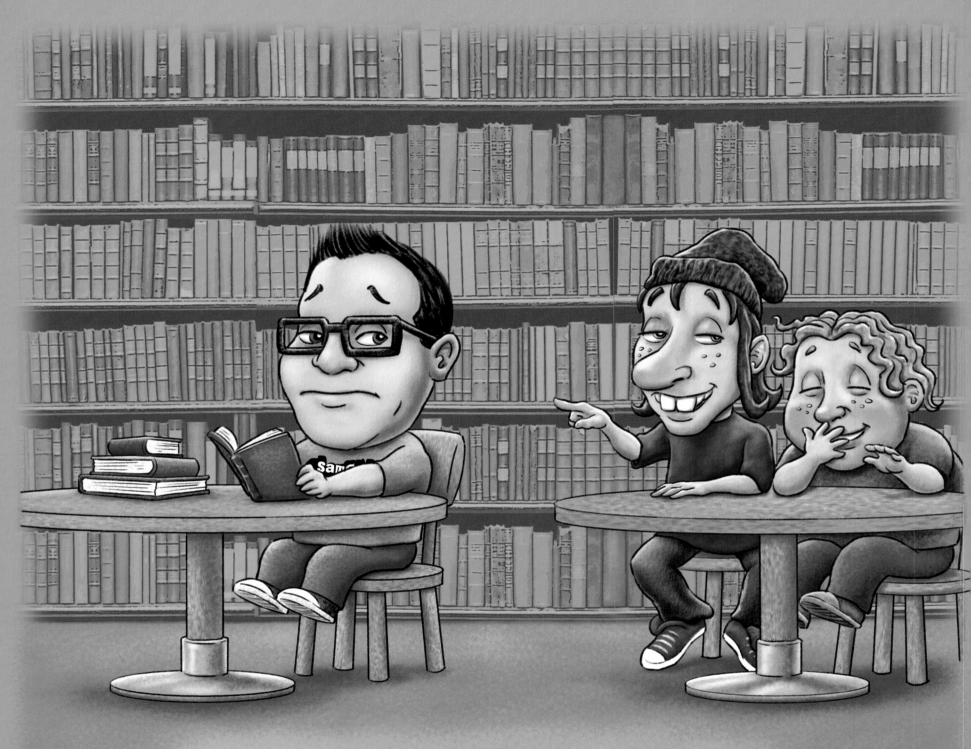

I also wear glasses. They help me to see.
Sometimes, though, people make fun of me.

Some people have differences
that make them feel stuck...
But being uncommon is a stroke of **good luck!**

Sometimes the thing that can make people sad
is also the thing that can make them feel glad.

It is your uniqueness that's really the seed.
Embrace it! Exploit it! And you will succeed.

To some people it's odd
to have no hair on your head,

But it saves so much time
when you get out of **bed!**

Some people keep quiet;
they don't like their voices.

**But it's just the thing
that can give them
some choices.**

Voice-over artist or motivational speaker...

how about talk show host, **comic** or middle school teacher?

Some people have birthmarks or scars on their face. It makes them self-conscious and feel out of place.

I'd show it with confidence,
tell my story with pride,
**And everyone would know
I have nothing to hide.**

I'd empower other people
to be who they are.

**Who knew so much good
could come just from a scar?**

Some people have freckles. Others wear braces.
We vary in sizes. And are of different races.

But no matter your race or what's on your face,
It's these things you embrace to carve out your place.

For all this to happen you must make a shift
and realize that "different" is truly a gift.

We all are unique in our own special way.
We all have our talents to work and to play.

You'll win the game when you start to believe
**that what makes you different
will help you achieve.**

WHAT'S UNIQUE ABOUT YOU

_____

_____

_____

_____

_____

_____

_____

_____

_____

ABOUT THE AUTHOR

Jimmy Vee is known around the world as the Five Foot High Marketing Guy. He has been creative since any one in his family can remember. He spends his days making stuff up and joking around (that's how his kids describe it).

Jimmy got his creative start by acting with action figures, building high tech gadgets out of ordinary household objects, playing made-up tunes on his trumpet and practicing the ancient arts of magic and ventriloquism.

In real life, Jimmy is the co-owner of an advertising and marketing agency and has co-authored numerous books on sales and marketing, including the bestseller *Gravitational Marketing: The Science of Attracting Customers*.

His agency has received numerous accolades and is recognized by INC. Magazine as one of fastest-growing private companies in America. His marketing campaigns have been heard all over the US and Canada and have even been featured by Ripley's Believe It Or Not.

Jimmy has dedicated his life to helping people discover what is unique about themselves and showing them how to capitalize on it. He is also one of the leading professional ventriloquists and kid show entertainers performing today.

Jimmy lives in Orlando, Florida with his wife, Christy, and their two children, Autumn and Vincent and a horde of ventriloquist dummies. This is his first children's book.

Find our more about Little Jimmy and the Same Is Lame® Foundation project at:

www.SameIsLame.com

Little Jimmy Says, "Same Is Lame"
Copyright © 2014 by James Venezio
Published by Atlas Press, LLC, Orlando, Florida

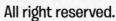

All right reserved.
No part of this book may be reproduced in any manner whatsoever without written permission except in
the case of brief quotations embodied in critical articles and reviews.
For information address Atlas Press, 3718 Avalon Park East Boulevard, Orlando, Fl 32828.
Same Is Lame® is a registered trademark of Scend, LLC.

Printed In The USA
Library of Congress-in-publication data is available
ISBN: 978-0-9854782-2-3

First Edition

Special thanks goes to my amazing wife, my brother, my mom, my dad and my biz partner/best bud for
their ever-present support.

The Shortest Man on the Flying Trapeze!